W9-DBH-201

Donated in memory of
Nettie Lou Holland
Custodian of West Georgia Regional Library Headquarters &
Neva Lomason Memorial Library, 1966-1980
by Edith G. Morehead
through the Friends of the Library
Matching Gift Program, 2006

WEST GA REG LIB SYS
Neva Lomason
Memorial Library

A BLUE BANNER
BIOGRAPHY

Beyoncé

By Kathleen Tracy

Mitchell Lane
PUBLISHERS

P.O. Box 196
Hockessin, Delaware 19707
Visit us on the web: www.mitchelllane.com
Comments? email us: mitchelllane@mitchelllane.com

Copyright © 2005 by Mitchell Lane Publishers. All rights reserved. No part of this book may be reproduced without written permission from the publisher. Printed and bound in the United States of America.

Printing   5   6   7   8   9

Blue Banner Biographies

Alicia Keys	Allen Iverson	Ashanti
Ashlee Simpson	Ashton Kutcher	Avril Lavigne
Beyoncé	Bow Wow	Britney Spears
Carrie Underwood	Christina Aguilera	Christopher Paul Curtis
Clay Aiken	Condoleezza Rice	Daniel Radcliffe
Derek Jeter	Eminem	Eve
Ja Rule	Jay-Z	Jennifer Lopez
J.K. Rowling	Jodie Foster	Justin Berfield
Kate Hudson	Lance Armstrong	Lindsay Lohan
Mario	Mary-Kate and Ashley Olsen	Melissa Gilbert
Michael Jackson	Missy Elliott	Nelly
P. Diddy	Paris Hilton	Queen Latifah
Ritchie Valens	Rita Williams-Garcia	Ron Howard
Rudy Giuliani	Sally Field	Selena
Shirley Temple	Usher	

Library of Congress Cataloging-in-Publication Data
Tracy, Kathleen.
     Beyoncé / Kathleen Tracy
         p. cm. - (A blue banner biography.)
     Includes discography (p.), filmography (p.), and index (p.).
     ISBN 1-58415-312-1 (library bound)
         1. Knowles, Beyoncé - Juvenile literature. 2. Singers - United States - Biography - Juvenile literature. I. Title. II. Series.
ML3930.K66T73 2004
782. 42164 ' 092 - dc22
                                       2004002046

ABOUT THE AUTHOR: Kathleen Tracy has been a journalist for over twenty years. Her writing has been featured in magazines including The Toronto Star's "Star Week", *A&E Biography* magazine, *KidScreen* and *TV Times*. She is also the author of numerous biographies including "The Boy Who Would be King" (Dutton), "Jerry Seinfeld" - The Entire Domain" (Carol Publishing), "Don Imus - America's Cowboy" (Carroll & Graf), "Mariano Guadalupe Vallejo," and "William Hewlett: Pioneer of the Computer Age," both for Mitchell Lane. She recently completed "God's Will?" for Sourcebooks.

PHOTO CREDITS: Cover: Bruno Vincent/Getty Images; p. 4 Bruno Vincent/Getty Images ; pp. 12, 18 Frank Micelotta & Staff/Getty Images; pp. 23, 24 Globe Photos; p. 28 Frederick M. Brown/Getty Images.

ACKNOWLEDGMENTS: The following story has been thoroughly researched, and to the best of our knowledge, represents a true story. While every possible effort has been made to ensure accuracy, the publisher will not assume liability for damages caused by inaccuracies in the data, and makes no warranty on the accuracy of the information contained herein. This story has not been authorized nor endorsed by Beyoncé Knowles.

CONTENTS

Through her success as a singer, songwriter and actress Beyoncé has emerged as one of the most popular and recognizable performers in the world. Although she enjoys meeting fans and being appreciated for her music, Beyoncé admits that being famous can make it difficult to find time to relax and just hang out with friends.

A Painful Lesson

*I*t was the biggest moment of Beyoncé Knowles's life. She found out that Girls Tyme, the six-girl singing group of which she was a member, was going to appear on national television. The show was called *Star Search.* Like *American Idol,* it gave young people from all over the country a chance to perform and to show off their talents. A panel of judges rated the performers. The winner had a chance to compete for the grand prize. Many famous performers appeared on *Star Search* as kids, including Christina Aguilera and Britney Spears. Both of them were asked to join the *Mickey Mouse Club* afterwards as a result of their performances.

Even though she was only 11 years old at the time, Beyoncé felt that she was ready to become famous. To get ready for the television show, she spent hours in her living room and backyard rehearsing with Girls Tyme. She and her father Mathew had formed the group.

Soon, the big day arrived and the girls went to the television studio. As they waited for their turn, they tried to keep calm by joking with each other. Each girl was very serious about performing well. Finally, it was time. They went on stage to face the judges. But instead of performing a song that showed off their ability to harmonize, they decided to do a rap song.

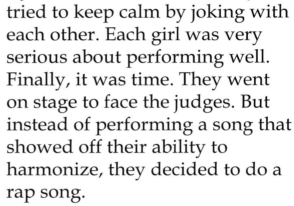

Instead of performing a song that showed their ability to harmonize, they decided to do a rap song.

"*Star Search* is a memorable moment," Beyoncé recalled in a Yahoo.com interview. "I was nine years old [actually, Beyoncé was 11 at the time] and we had been rehearsing forever—it seemed like a hundred years for a 9-year-old. We were so young, but were dedicated, and we were very, very hungry. Something inside of us, even at nine years old, was like, This is fun, we love it, we want to do it, and we had supportive parents who allowed us to rehearse on the weekends and took us to these performances—all of that stuff helped.

"But the song we did was not good; we did the wrong song. When they said they gave us three stars, we were forcing a smile because we lost. We couldn't even last until we got backstage; the tears were already falling. We were devastated; we thought our lives were over. It definitely humbles you. That was my first time I lost something that I really wanted to win, which is great for a person sometimes. Sometimes things don't go exactly how you planned and those things make you stronger. That was my first struggle, and my first hurdle that I had to jump over. We just said, OK, something's not right, we have to work hard. And we overcame that even at nine years old, which I'm very proud of."

Beyoncé's dad, Mathew, was also stunned that his daughter had not impressed the judges. He asked the show's producer for some advice. The producer told him not to give up hope.

"You know, Mr. Knowles, those who have lost are the ones who go on to success," the producer continued, as Mathew recalled to *Ebony* magazine. "For those who lose, something happens. They go back and rededicate themselves, reorganize and some of them go on to make it. For some reason, those who win don't go on."

> *"That was my first time I lost something that I really wanted to win, which is great for a person sometimes."*

The producer was right. Beyoncé learned a valuable lesson from her *Star Search* defeat — if she really wanted to be a professional singer she had to completely dedicate herself to making that dream come true. In just a few years, her hard work would pay off. She would succeed beyond her wildest dreams.

Born to Sing

*B*eyoncé Giselle Knowles was born September 4, 1981, at Park Plaza Hospital in Houston, Texas. Her dad Mathew was a medical equipment salesman and her mom Tina owned Headliners Hair Salon. Although they weren't rich, Beyoncé's parents worked hard. She grew up in a nice home. She and her sister Solange, who is almost five years younger, attended private schools and grew up loving music because it was an important part of the Knowles's household. Both Mathew and Tina sang in high school and participated in many talent shows. Although they never pursued careers as performers, they still enjoyed music. One of the girls' favorite family activities was to sit around the piano and sing with their mom while Mathew played.

By the time Beyoncé was in first grade, she had already decided she wanted to be a professional singer.

Her parents saw her perform when she was seven years old. Mathew and Tina quickly realized that their daughter had a special talent.

"I sang in my elementary school talent show, and the second I stepped on the stage, I transformed into something else," Beyoncé told Alisha Fisher of CNN's Headline News. "My parents were like, Who is that little girl? That's not Beyoncé. And I fell in love with performing."

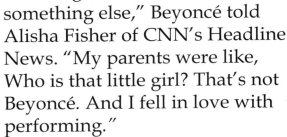

"I sang in my elementary school talent show, and the second I stepped on the stage, I transformed into something else."

The song she sang was "Imagine." Mathew was so impressed with Beyoncé's talent that he encouraged his daughter to form a group, which eventually became Girls Tyme.

After their disappointing appearance on Star Search, Mathew realized changes had to be made. The six-member group disbanded. The new group consisted of Beyoncé, her friend LaTavia Roberson—whom she had met two years earlier while auditioning for another children's group—and Beyoncé's cousin Kelly Rowland. LeToya Luckett joined them in 1993. Over the next several years they performed under a number of names, including Something Fresh, Cliché, and The

Dolls. The girls would rehearse while Mathew watched and offered suggestions.

"We'd rehearse every week and we'd go to my mom's salon, Headliners, to test out our new songs on all of her customers," Beyoncé said in a BeatBoxBetty.com interview. "We'd get tips too! My best memories are in that salon— sweeping up hair and trying to be all grown up on the phone like I was a receptionist." The girls performed as often as they could and soon began earning a lot of fans in Houston.

Beyoncé soon discovered that she was happiest when she was singing. Whenever she was on stage performing, she felt as if she belonged.

"I loved being on the stage," she told Paul Fischer in an interview in *Film Monthly*. "I felt that I could express myself and perform and do what was in my heart on the stage. I felt comfortable on the stage."

> *Beyoncé discovered she was happiest when she was singing. Whenever she was on stage she felt she belonged.*

It was a very different story at school. Beyoncé refers to herself as a shy and unpopular "geek" who wore braces and glasses.

"No one would have believed that my mom owned her own beauty salon, because I went out of my way not to look too pretty," Beyoncé admitted in her autobiography, *Soul Survivors: The Official Autobiography of Destiny's Child.* "I did everything I could to not draw attention to myself."

Even her now-famous name was the source of embarrassment.

"The deal my parents made before I was born was that my dad would pick my middle name and my mom would choose my first name," she explained in *Soul*

Mathew, Tina, and Solange Knowles attend the 35th Annual NAACP Image Awards on March 6, 2004 in Hollywood, California where Beyoncé received the Entertainer of the Year award.

Survivors. "So Beyoncé comes from her — it's actually her maiden name. Through the years, I have grown to love it, but when I was little, it was just another reason for kids to pick on me. Every morning when the teacher would take roll call, I wanted to crawl under my desk. I never felt like I fit in completely with kids my age. I felt uncomfortable with a lot of attention."

While she might have disliked being noticed in school, on stage she basked in the attention. Before too long, Beyoncé and the other three girls would suddenly find themselves in the national spotlight.

Beyoncé's name was a source of embarrassment when she was in school. But through the years she has grown to love it.

Early Struggles

Soon after the appearance on *Star Search*, Beyoncé's father decided to devote himself full time to her career. Convinced that his daughter had the talent and the drive to succeed as a singer, Mathew quit his sales job to become Destiny's Child's full-time manager.

"My father became our manager when we were eleven and twelve, and he would always book shows for us," Beyoncé told *Ebony* magazine. "We would try to perform once a week, and in the summer, twice a week. I'm very lucky. Both my parents support me and my career."

Beyoncé knew that her family had made a huge sacrifice. It wasn't easy. In order to make ends meet on just the money Tina earned, Beyoncé's parents sold their home and cars. The family moved into an apartment.

While Mathew managed the group, Tina acted as their stylist, making their costumes and doing their hair before performances. Between Mathew's skills as a salesman and the girls' talent, Destiny's Child began getting hired to open for big-name acts such as Dru Hill when they performed in Houston.

Surprisingly, Beyoncé kept her singing a secret at school.

"People thought I was stuck-up…because I was quiet," she recalled in her autobiography. "Some people misunderstand quietness and shyness; they think you're full of yourself. They don't even give you a chance. With those two strikes against me already, there was no way that I was about to let anyone in school know I could sing! That would just make things worse."

"People thought I was stuck-up because I was quiet. Some people misunderstand quietness and shyness."

Beyoncé's days were filled with activity from early morning to late at night. She attended Houston's High School for the Performing and Visual Arts. Then she would come home and rehearse, sometimes for as long as eight hours.

As a young girl, Beyoncé says she was chubby. Mathew felt it was important for a performer to look

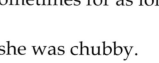

her best. He started his daughter on a health and exercise program. Before school in the mornings she would go for a three-mile jog. She also ate a healthy diet that consisted mostly of soup and skinless chicken breasts.

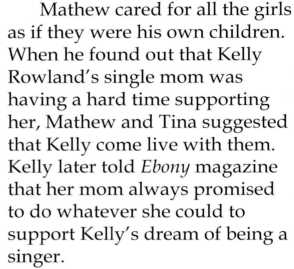

Beyoncé started a health and exercise program because it's important for a performer to look her best.

Mathew cared for all the girls as if they were his own children. When he found out that Kelly Rowland's single mom was having a hard time supporting her, Mathew and Tina suggested that Kelly come live with them. Kelly later told *Ebony* magazine that her mom always promised to do whatever she could to support Kelly's dream of being a singer.

"I think my mom is a really strong person, and I'm just blessed to have three parents in my life," Kelly said. "Tina and Mathew have been like my mother and father. I call them my aunt and uncle."

As for Beyoncé, Kelly added, "Our relationship goes deeper than Destiny's Child. That's my sister, and I love her and I know she feels the same way about me. We have each other's back, no matter what."

His determination was rewarded when they signed a record deal in 1995. Beyoncé and her parents were ecstatic. But their happiness was short-lived. Just a few months later, the label dropped the group with no warning. The girls were devastated but Mathew refused to let them give up. He continued trying to get the girls another deal.

His hard work paid off. In 1997, they signed with Columbia Records. They decided to call the group Destiny's Child, from a Biblical passage in the Book of Isaiah.

They got their first big break with "Killing Time." It was part of the soundtrack for the film *Men in Black*, starring Will Smith and Tommy Lee Jones. A short time later, Beyoncé moved to Los Angeles to start working on their first album, which was called *Destiny's Child*.

The group's first single from Destiny's Child, "No, No, No" was released in 1998 when Beyoncé was 16. The first time she heard the song on the radio was a moment she would never forget. She and her parents were picking Solange up from school.

> *They decided to call the group Destiny's Child, from a Biblical passage in the Book of Isaiah.*

Beyoncé performs at the 46th Annual Grammy Awards held at the Staples Center on February 8, 2004 in Los Angeles, California.

"She and all her friends were walking out, and the song started playing," Beyoncé told *Launch*. "It was unbelievable. We jumped out and started running around the car. We screamed and laughed and cried and danced and sang and all of that. My sister was so embarrassed. And then she heard the song, and she's like, 'Aaaahhhh!' And she dropped her bag and started running around the car too."

A few months later a bigger surprise came when Whitney Houston invited the girls to her birthday party in New York.

"We got some money and put our happy butts on that plane and went straight to that party. We even dressed alike, like we were going to perform. And Whitney came and hugged us, and she said that she loved us. We were just in awe," Beyoncé told *Launch*.

Also in 1998, Destiny's Child won three awards at Soul Train Lady of Soul Awards. It all seemed too good to be true. Unfortunately it was. Just as they were poised for stardom, Destiny's Child would be torn apart in a fight over money.

> *In 1998, Destiny's Child won three awards at Soul Train Lady of Soul Awards.*

Overcoming
Adversity

*J*ust as their second album was being released, Beyoncé and Kelly were stunned. Beyoncé's longtime friends LaTavia Roberson and LeToya Luckett abruptly quit the group in early 2000 and filed a lawsuit against Mathew Knowles. The two girls accused Mathew of mismanaging the group's money and trying to present Beyoncé as the "star" of the group, rather than promoting all the girls equally. Beyoncé was emotionally devastated. It felt as if her family was breaking up and she sunk into a painful depression. According to friends, she barely left her bedroom for a month.

While Beyoncé struggled to overcome losing her friends, Mathew responded by immediately hiring two new singers—Michelle Williams and Farrah Franklin— to replace LaTavia and LeToya. In the music video for "Say My Name," Michelle and Farrah lip-synch to the voices of LaTavia and LeToya. Then Beyoncé was stunned again when Farrah announced she was quitting after only five months with the group. She said that she couldn't handle the long hours Mathew made them work and rehearse.

Instead of hiring a replacement for Farrah, Destiny's Child became a trio.

Eventually, LeToya's and LaTavia's lawsuit was settled out of court. It remained a difficult time for Beyoncé because rumors were swirling that she was to blame for the break-up. "I can sit here all day and say I am not a diva, but it won't matter, because people just have to be around us and see how we support each other," she said in the *Launch* interview. "That's how a group is supposed to be."

Instead of getting depressed again, Beyoncé went back to work. She wrote and produced much of the reformed group's next album, appropriately called *Survivor*. Released in 2001, the album debuted at #1 and would go on to sell more than nine million copies worldwide. In addition to proving that the new-look Destiny's Child was as popular as ever, the album's success also established

> *Beyoncé wrote and produced most of the album "Survivor." Released in 2001, the album debuted at #1.*

Beyoncé as a songwriter as well as a singer. That same year, Destiny's Child took home two Grammy awards: Best R&B song and Best R&B performance by a Duo or Group for "Say My Name." They also won five *Billboard* Awards including Artist of the Year.

The album "Survivor" was a turning point for Destiny's Child. All three girls had been offered the chance to do solo albums.

Survivor, which included the hit single "Independent Women Part 1" from the soundtrack for the film *Charlie's Angels*, was a turning point for Destiny's Child. Although Michelle was new to the group, Kelly and Beyoncé had been singing together over half their lives. All three girls had been offered the chance to do solo albums and they decided to take a break from the group to pursue individual projects. The time also allowed Beyoncé the opportunity to go on acting auditions. After appearing in an MTV movie based on the opera *Carmen*, Beyoncé was surprised to get a starring role in *Austin Powers in Goldmember*. She played the role of Foxxy Cleopatra opposite Mike Myers, who portrayed Austin Powers.

Beyoncé admitted she never thought she would get the part. She was very nervous during her first few days on the set. "I didn't know what I was doing, " she said in a beatboxbetty.com interview. "I was just grateful to get the opportunity. I didn't think what would happen if it would go bad, I just did it and tried to do the best I could. I tried to learn. I felt like it was a new chapter of my life, a new way to grow as an artist."

Her excitement at being in a movie was dampened when Beyoncé learned that LeToya and LaTavia were again suing Destiny's Child. They claimed that lyrics in

Beyoncé made her film debut opposite Mike Meyers in the 2002 comedy, Austin Powers in Goldmember. In the movie, she played Foxxy Cleopatra, who helps Powers save the world from Dr. Evil.

the song "Survivor" (one of the big single hits from the album of the same name) violated part of their legal agreement not to speak badly about each other.

Despite LaTavia Roberson and LeToya Luckett's decision to leave the group, Destiny's Child has continued to achieve great success as the trio of Beyoncé, Kelly Rowland and Michelle Williams, with their Survivor Album has sold over six million copies worldwide.

Beyoncé was hurt. "It's really unfortunate that when you get successful, people try to steal your happiness," she said in her *Launch* interview. "But they can't….It's just sad. I don't want no drama, I don't want no enemies. All I want to do is go into the studio, write my music, do my movies and perform. I'm not trying to hurt nobody, offend nobody. I'm just happy to be here, and it's just sad that all this other stuff comes along with it."

But nothing could take away from Beyoncé's excitement at seeing herself in a movie. "The premiere was the first time I saw the movie," she told the British website icnetwork. "It was really weird to see myself that big. But I was happy and relieved because I had been so nervous about it and I was like, Wow, that's really cool. I was proud."

> **Nothing could take away from Beyoncé's excitement at seeing herself in a movie.**

After the movie, Beyoncé turned her attention to her solo album. Once again she wrote or co-wrote most of the songs. Many people questioned if Beyoncé could be as successful on her own as she was with Destiny's Child. The album *Dangerously in Love* would provide the answer.

A Bright Future

*E*verything came together for Beyoncé in 2003. In May, her first solo single, "Crazy in Love," was released. By the end of the year, she had sold more than two million copies of the album *Dangerously In Love*. She starred in her second movie, *The Fighting Temptations*, and it was revealed she was dating rapper Jay-Z. In December, she learned she had been nominated for six Grammys, more than any other performer. A couple of days later, Beyoncé walked off with four *Billboard* Awards, including New Female Artist of the Year and new R&B artist of the year.

During her acceptance speech, she said, "This is amazing! I want to first thank God for blessing me with all of these beautiful opportunities and wonderful people that I've been surrounded with. This has been an incredible year. I want to thank all my fans, and thank my sister Solange — I love you."

It was a year she could never forget. "It seems like every month something really huge happened," she told *Entertainment Weekly*, which voted her one of the top 10 entertainers of the year. And she shows little signs of slowing down. She has plans for a clothing line, a second solo album and another Destiny's Child album in the works.

Despite her hectic life, Beyoncé says she doesn't feel pressure or stress. "I don't think about it; I just do my own thing," she told Sam Kent on handbag.com. "I love what I do. There are certain things that come along with it that I don't like, but it's a part of my job. Nobody's job is perfect. People are really critical in general and it's ten times worse when you're under the microscope, so it's hard to grow up under that. But I have people who love me regardless of whether I sell another record or not."

> *Despite her hectic life, Beyoncé says she doesn't feel pressure or stress.*

Although she lives in the spotlight, with reporters and photographers following her around, Beyoncé has managed to keep her privacy. "I've always been a private person," she observed to Kent. "When I was at school I didn't tell people I was in a group. Not because I was ashamed of it, just because

Beyoncé poses with her six Grammys backstage in the Pressroom at the 46th Annual Grammy Awards held at the Staples Center on February 8, 2004 in Los Angeles, California.

I'm private. I'll tell my friends, but I just don't feel comfortable telling the whole world."

Beyoncé does say she's looking forward to one day getting married and having children of her own. Despite her increasing fame, Beyoncé, who has a strong belief in God and attends church, has not let it go to her head. In fact, there are times she longs for a simpler life.

"I still like roller coasters, talking on the phone and being silly," she told Paul Fischer in a *Film Monthly* interview. "I like when people are silly because then I can be silly."

There are also times Beyoncé thinks about the sacrifices she made to be a singer.

Beyoncé says she wouldn't change her life. I love what I do and I love to perform; that's what fuels me.

"I had a tutor, which is very serious and boring, nor was I ever a cheerleader or went to games or any of those things, so when I'm able to, I want to do stuff that is fun. I've had the responsibility since I was 15 of someone who is 25 or 30, so now I have a lot of pressure. I make a lot of adult decisions, and that has forced me to grow up a little faster," she added.

Even so, she told Fischer that she wouldn't change her life. "I love what I do and I love to perform; that's what fuels me."

1981	Born on September 4 in Houston, Texas
1986	Sister Solange is born
1989	Wins first place in school talent contest
1990	Meets LaTavia Roberson at an audition
1991	Joins new all-girl group called Girls Tyme
1992	Appears on *Star Search* with Girls Tyme
1997	Signs record deal with Columbia
1998	Releases first album, *Destiny's Child*
1998	Wins three Soul Train Awards for *Destiny's Child*
2000	LaTavia Roberson and LeToya Luckett leave Destiny's Child
2001	*Survivor* debuts as number one album
2001	Wins two Grammys with Destiny's Child for Best R&B Song and Best R&B performance
2001	Wins ASCAP Pop Songwriter of the Year award
2001	Makes professional acting debut in MTV's *Carmen: A HipHopera*
2002	Co-stars opposite Mike Meyers in *Austin Powers in Goldmember*
2003	Releases first solo album, *Dangerously In Love*
2003	Is nominated for six Grammys for "Dangerously in Love"
2003	Wins MTV awards for Best Female Video, Best R&B Video and Best Choreography in a Video for "Crazy in Love"
2004	Wins six Grammy awards
2004	Is awarded Entertainer of the Year award at the NAACP Image Awards

FOR FURTHER READING

Gittins, Ian. *Destiny's Child*. London: Carlton Books, 2002.

Kenyatta, Kelly. *Destiny's Child*. Hollywood, California: Busta Books, 2001.

Knowles, Beyoncé, Kelly Rowland and Michelle Williams. *Soul Survivors: The Official Autobiography of Destiny's Child*. New York: Regan Books, 2002.

Knowles, Tina. *Destiny's Style*. New York: Regan Books, 2002.

Rodway, Keith. *Destiny's Child: The Unauthorised Biography in Words and Pictures*. London: Chrome Dreams, 2001.

On the Internet

http://www.beyonceonline.com

http://www.beyonce-knowles.com

http://www.1greatcelebsite.com/beyonce_knowles/ interview.htm

http://www.superiorpics.com/destinys_child/interviews.html

DISCOGRAPHY

1998	*Destiny's Child*
2000	*The Writing's On The Wall*
2001	*Survivor*
2001	*8 Days of Christmas*
2002	*This Is The Remix*
2003	*Dangerously In Love*
2004	*Live at Wembley*

FILMOGRAPHY

2001	*Carmen: A Hip Hopera* (TV)
2002	*Austin Powers in Goldmember*
2002	*The Victoria's Secret Fashion Show* (TV)
2003	*The Fighting Temptations*
2005	*The Pink Panther*

INDEX

Beyonce /
J Knowles TRA 31057010079351

Tracy, Kathleen.
WEST GA REGIONAL LIBRARY SYS